TIPS

Retirement for Music Educators

Compiled by
A. Verne Wilson

Past National Chairman
MENC Committee for
Retired Music Educators

Music Educators National Conference

ISBN 0-940796-59-7

Foreword

The Music Educators National Conference (MENC) has created the TIPS series to provide music educators with a variety of ideas on a wide range of practical subjects. Each TIPS booklet is a compilation of methods, ideas, and suggestions that have proved valuable to many music educators. MENC has developed this quick-reference series to be used as a starting point for creating and adapting projects for your particular situation.

TIPS: Retirement for Music Educators is designed for retired music educators (and those about to retire) who need some specific suggestions on how to live a healthier, happier, and more satisfying life after retirement.

No one grows old by merely living a number of years. People grow old by deserting their ideas. You are as young as your faith, as old as your doubt, as young as your self-confidence, as old as your fears, as young as your hope, as old as your despair.

Anonymous

Table of Contents

Before Retirement

If you were planning to spend the rest of your life in another country, you would want to learn as much about it as possible. You would read books about the climate, people, history, and architecture. You would talk to people who had lived there. You might even learn a bit of its language. Old age is like another country. You'll enjoy it more if you have prepared yourself before you go.

B. F. Skinner and Margaret Vaughn, 20.[1]

* * *

Sit down, with your spouse if you are married, and plan ahead carefully for those retirement years even though you may still be in the middle of your career. Remember that those classified as senior citizens are getting both younger (because of early retirement) and older (because of the increase in the average life span). The increasing numbers on both ends of the scale mean that your period of retirement may approximate the number of years you were employed.

* * *

Decide when you want to retire. Social Security benefits are generally available at age sixty-five, although one may draw them at a reduced rate as early as sixty-two. Your state or local retirement program (school pension) may be available, also at a reduced rate, as early as age fifty-five. It might not, however, include the prepaid health plan that you now receive from your employer, and Medicare is not available until age sixty-five. For this reason, and given that retirement is no longer required at age sixty-five, you may decide to continue working.

Estimate as accurately as possible what your economic situation will be after you retire. An estimate of your total income will include:
- Pensions for yourself and for your spouse: The local office of your state pension plan can tell you the distribution formula and how it will affect your pension payments depending on when you wish to retire.

---

1. Full citations for sources of quotations, unless provided in the text, can be found in the Bibliography.

- Social Security for yourself and for your spouse: The local Social Security office can give you accurate estimates along with many free brochures that contain information about the Social Security and Medicare systems.
- Other incomes: Some examples are certificates of deposit, individual retirement accounts, stocks, rental property, and investments such as securities and mutual funds.

An estimate of your total expenses will include:
- Housing: This includes mortgage payments or rent, utilities, insurance, upkeep, improvements, and replacements.
- Clothing and personal needs
- Food
- Transportation: This includes costs associated with a car, such as maintenance, insurance, and gas, or public transportation costs.
- Entertainment and travel
- Gifts and contributions
- Taxes: Consider all taxes, including property, sales, and federal and state income taxes. (You need to know if a portion of your Social Security benefits will be taxed by the federal government and possibly by your state government and whether your pension will be taxed by the state.)
- Health care: Contact local health agencies, and compare the various programs they offer as well as the cost of each; then select the one that best meets your needs. Make sure you are insured for the costs not covered by Medicare. You may also want to insure yourself for nursing home care.
- Miscellaneous expenses

If, after estimating your retirement income and expenses, you think your income will not be sufficient, you can increase your income by cutting expenses, working more years before retirement, or taking a job after retirement. A professional finance planner can assist you in working out an investment program.

Attend financial planning workshops and seminars. Some are offered free of charge to groups of educators. Some have been held at MENC division and national conferences. Ask your state music education association to include one at its next meeting.

* * *

Decide where you want to live after you retire. Psychologists generally agree that it is best to stay in the general area in which you have lived and worked because of close ties to family, friends, and colleagues. If you think, however, that you would like to move to another location, try it out in advance. Before selling your home and moving to another part of the country, spend a couple of weeks there in a motel. Visit at different times of the year. If you have decided to undertake any other large-scale commitments, consider the pros and cons before making the final decision. If you have planned to buy a recreational vehicle to tour the country for a year, try renting one for two or three weeks and make a shorter trip.

* * *

Set some goals regarding how you want to spend your retirement time. Focus on your talents and abilities instead of looking at the handicaps that may come with the aging process. Retiring to the old rocking chair and watching television all day is not a satisfactory option; it can lead to early "rust out." Goals could include setting aside daily time for physical exercise, helping others, community service, social activities, and some private, quiet activities.

* * *

Be prepared for change and learn to *handle change positively*. As John Naisbitt predicted in his book, *Megatrends* (New York: Warner Books, 1982), the amount of information passed around in our society seems to be doubling every few years. In this age of instant communication, change is inevitable: not only the change around us, but physical changes within us as we grow older.

* * *

Be sure your intentions are clearly stated in writing. If you have not already prepared your will, consult a lawyer who can help you ensure that your property will be distributed exactly as you wish. Name someone to be executor of your estate.

Know the laws of your state regarding estate taxes. Your attorney can give you this information, and the financial planning workshops mentioned earlier can provide much assistance in this area.

Know the ramifications of joint accounts and joint ownerships. These ramifications can vary from state to state. Understand what the various forms of accounts and ownership mean, and be sure that they are doing what you intended. For example, if you put your assets into a joint account with one of your grown children and he or she dies before you do, you might end up paying taxes on your own assets. Make sure that the beneficiaries named on your insurance policies are those you want, and make sure that this information is kept up-to-date.

You may want to name someone to be your deputy and give this person access to your safety deposit vault without giving him or her joint ownership. For more information about these subjects, you may need to consult an attorney.

If your state recognizes a "living will," which is a statement of your wishes should you no longer be able to make decisions affecting your future, you may want to consider making one. A copy of this living will should be sent to your family, your attorney, your doctor, and your spiritual adviser.

Understand the use of power of attorney and durable power of attorney, and name someone who can pay bills and handle your business if you should become temporarily disabled. Attention to these details can help you achieve security and peace of mind in your retirement.

* * *

[There] is a need to prepare people in early life to meet the challenges which will inevitably be theirs.

Mary Baird Carlsen, 234.

* * *

the small society

I'VE BEEN GIVING SOME SERIOUS THOUGHT TO RETIRING—

THEN I'D BETTER GIVE SOME SERIOUS THOUGHT TO GETTING A JOB—

Yates — BRICKMAN

During Retirement

The more interests people have, the better their lives are, especially after retirement. They don't ever retire from life. They retire from one job and move on to others that are frequently more interesting and more rewarding than the profession they've left.

Joyce Brothers, "Ask Dr. Brothers,"
This Week, 15 May 1985, C10.

* * *

Don't retire from life. Keep in touch with the world, and stay a well-informed citizen. Read the daily newspapers. Listen to and watch news programs on both local radio and television broadcasts. Subscribe to and read magazines such as *Time, Newsweek,* or *U.S. News and World Report.* Maintain contact with friends and colleagues to help keep up-to-date on what is going on in the world about you.

* * *

Maintain good health. Have your doctor give you regular physical checkups. Permit him or her to advise you on how best to manage your blood pressure and cholesterol levels. Consult with him or her about your nutritional needs, your weight control, and your exercise program. If you take medication, take it as prescribed by your doctor. If you smoke, ask your doctor for help to stop smoking. Consider joining a health maintenance organization if there is one in your community. Its focus is to help you stay healthy—not to wait until something breaks down.

Much new knowledge has become available recently about nutrition, and more research is needed on this subject. A diet, however, that contains less fat, sugar, and salt along with more fruits, vegetables, and grains will certainly prove to be helpful.

Develop weight control. Consult with your doctor to establish an acceptable body weight. Weigh yourself regularly to determine whether your weight is above or below the acceptable level. If you are overweight, adjust your food intake to help eliminate excess body fat, which puts a strain on the action of the heart and other body functions. Guard against undereating, because this can result in both loss of body weight and an increasing vulnerability to physical disorders and distresses. You should not eat or snack between meals and should not overdose yourself with vitamin and mineral supplements.

Now that you have more time for exercise, be careful about starting a vigorous exercise program if you are out of shape. Walking at a brisk, constant pace on a regular basis seems to be one of the best ways to strengthen muscles, tone the whole body, burn calories, control weight, and help ensure a general sense of well-being. Some people enjoy walking in malls because it allows them to be inside while walking a predetermined distance. During cold and stormy weather, you can use an exercise bicycle on a daily basis as a substitute for walking.

Have your eyes checked regularly, and get new glasses or contacts when needed. Modern medical science, which has developed new techniques in cataract surgery and other treatments of visual problems, is helping senior citizens keep good eyesight longer and longer.

Give attention to your ears. Your hearing may not be as sharp as it once was, but this can be corrected, helping not only you but those around you.

See your dentist regularly. New procedures have been developed in dentistry that help people keep their own teeth. This will help you retain the pleasure of eating and continue good nutritional habits.

* * *

Develop a continuity in your everyday activities. Maintain some sort of routine. As a music educator you know the value of rhythm. There are bodily and physical rhythms that help us keep an easy flow in our daily lives. It is not necessary to continue the same heavy daily schedule that was a part of your preretirement living, but having some constructive things to do regularly, such as tending a garden, driving for meals-on-wheels, or tutoring a child (done on a regular basis) is one way to overcome the "old rocking chair" syndrome and can lead to a more interesting and satisfying life.

* * *

Because some problems cannot be solved in old ways (and boredom is one of them), it becomes important to stimulate new activity and interest. Novelty, deliberate change, and new learning are essential for older persons. The challenge is to keep creatively busy.

Mary Baird Carlsen, 240.

* * *

Continue to spend time improving your skills and developing your interests. Consider enrolling in courses at a nearby college, university, or community college. Some of these institutions offer free tuition to those ages sixty-two and older. You might take courses in areas other than music that have particular appeal to you. Many local senior centers offer classes in crafts and hobbies, and local libraries often offer discussion-group series about classics or current books.

Investigate the worldwide course offerings of the popular Elderhostel program (headquarters address: 80 Boylston Street, Suite 400, Boston 02116), which is a major source of educational and recreational opportunities for senior Americans who desire to remain intellectually active either by teaching courses or by taking them in this country and abroad. For retired persons who enjoy traveling but are not interested in study, there are travel agencies that specialize in providing guided tours for senior citizens. One such aid is the travel service provided by the American Association of Retired Persons (AARP). (Write to P.O. Box 38997, Los Angeles 90038.) This organization offers AARP members special rates for guided tours to exotic places all over the world. Now is the time when you can explore a new interest or a new hobby or visit new places you did not have time to see during your working years.

* * *

Consider writing your memoirs, making them as lengthy and detailed or as brief as you wish. You may find it highly rewarding to reflect on parents, family, personal experiences, people who influenced your life, education, travels, what led you to your career in music education, and highlights of that career. Seeing where you have been and what you have accomplished will help you set goals for a meaningful and creative retirement. Your family will be grateful to you for taking the time and energy to make these very personal thoughts and information available to them.

* * *

> Memory serves our sense of identity: it provides continuity, wisdom and serenity. . . . Goethe noted that "he is the happiest man who can see the connection between the end and the beginning of his life." The act of recall can renew our awareness of the present and restore our sense of wonder.
>
> Robert Butler, quoted in Mary Baird Carlsen, 239.

* * *

Maintain active involvement in the Music Educators National Conference by becoming an active retired member. Continue to participate in the MENC division and state organizations. If your state association is divided into districts, take part in the district group as well. Plan to attend the national, division, and state conferences.

* * *

Continue your membership in local, state, and national organizations such as your church or synagogue and in local civic and social organizations. Some local communities and states offer organizations that provide retirees with opportunities to exchange ideas and to be of service to the community.

* * *

If you are not presently a member of the American Association of Retired Persons (AARP), consider becoming a member. Membership is open to persons ages fifty and older. This association speaks eloquently for the rights of retired people, and it is the leading guardian and spokesman in protecting those rights. Some of the privileges of membership in AARP are reduced rates for life, home, and auto insurance; reduced rates at hotels and motels across the country; reduced rates on auto rentals; and reduced rates on some other travel costs. Members also receive *Modern Maturity*, the association's bimonthly magazine, which helps keep members aware of current conditions affecting senior citizens. Nonprofit pharmacy services, news bulletins, and representation in Washington, D.C., are also parts of the AARP program. To join, write the American Association of Retired Persons, Membership Processing Center, P.O. Box 199, Long Beach, California 90801.

* * *

Engage in social activities such as square dancing, ballroom dancing, bridge, golf, or bowling. Share your music talents by playing in a local music group or singing in a community or church choir.

Take part in programs that enhance the development of your creative abilities, such as performing or composing music. Writing articles for publication on topics such as the importance of music in the lives of individuals can contribute to the development of your creative skills. Giving talks about understanding and appreciating music performances are other ways to enhance the development of both your creative abilities and those of your listeners.

Do not become withdrawn from family, friends, or society. Do not let your interests become static.

* * *

Everybody. . . should be doing something about which he cares deeply. And if he is to escape the prison of self, it must be something not essentially egocentric in nature.

John W. Gardner, 16–17.

* * *

the small society

HOO-BOY!

RETIREMENT SURE TAKES ALL THE FUN OUT OF WEEKENDS!

Yates — BRICKMAN

Sharing Your Talent and Expertise

With a frequently untapped wealth of competencies and experiences, older people have much to give. This fact, coupled with fewer requirements for their time, gives them unique opportunity to assume special kinds of helping roles.

Mary Baird Carlsen, 237.

* * *

Plan to share your expertise, energy, and time with others. Not only will this enrich your own life; it will strengthen bonds with others. Make yourself available to beginning music educators, and help them become more effective teachers. You can extend this availability to more experienced music educators who may be suffering from "burnout." After establishing rapport with the teacher, visit his or her class and evaluate the problem before offering suggestions for improving the situation. Presenting workshops and seminars to music teachers faced with problems can also be helpful.

* * *

Volunteer to spend time each week helping a child or several children have a rich musical experience. Give private music lessons to young people and adults in the community. Provide opportunities for them to share their music skills by playing for each other and for other members of the community. Provide opportunities for the students to perform together as an ensemble. This will help them develop their interests and skills.

* * *

Organize and direct a music program at a senior center or in a retirement community. The program could include a choral or an instrumental group, sing-alongs, or a class in music appreciation that would focus on developing music understanding through better listening skills. If some of the community residents have tickets to local symphony orchestra concerts or opera performances, they would certainly welcome a preview of the music that will be performed.

Organize music activities for residents in a nursing home. Some of the residents may be trained musicians, and others may have a strong interest in music. They will appreciate your thoughtfulness and efforts to bring music back into their lives. Two possible activities are leading a sing-along with some of the residents, using rhythm instruments to accompany the singing, or bringing school groups to perform for the residents. Again, residents can be asked to join in on some of the numbers. "Silver Tones among the Gold" by Howard A. Doolin (published by Rhythm Band) is an excellent source of materials for this kind of music activity.

* * *

Become the director of music for a church. Develop a music program for church members of all ages: Involve the whole extended family. A variety of choral programs that involve singers of different ages and abilities should be a part of the total program. Your program could also include instrumental groups such as bell choirs (at different levels of proficiency) and other instrumental ensembles.

* * *

If there is to be a retired MENC members' chorus or orchestra performance at a national or division MENC conference, make plans to become a member of the group that interests you most. Remember that music has strong social and recreational values as well as aesthetic values.

* * *

Support local school and community music programs by attending their concerts. If these organizations offer memberships, make a contribution and become a member.

All of us have a need to be wanted. By being of service to others, both young and old, we can satisfy this need through music.

* * *

Being an Articulate Advocate

Become an advocate for music and the other arts. You, as a retired music educator, are well aware that aesthetic experiences improve the quality of life. You are sensitive to the importance of music as a means of enhancing aesthetic expression. Because of your background, verbal skills, and active involvement in music education, you can be an effective communicator in informing the community about the need for maintaining high-quality music education programs in the schools.

* * *

For ideas and suggestions about how to become a more effective spokesman for high-quality music and music education programs, confer with other retired music educators who are serving as role models. There should be a general sharing of ideas and suggestions.

Help achieve high-quality music programs for all students in your locale by keeping in touch with music educators in the schools. Issues such as the importance of music as a basic part of education, the need to forestall the cutting back of music programs because of financial problems, or the problems caused for music programs by the addition of more curriculum requirements are topics that you, the retired music educator, can address successfully.

* * *

Accept invitations to speak about music and music education at meetings of the PTA, civic clubs, church groups, and other organizations. Always emphasize the importance of having high-quality music education programs available for today's youth. Some topics you could use to show why a definitive contact with music is so important are "Why Music Is Important in the Development of a Better Life," "Why Music Is a

Basic and Not a Frill," and "How Music Played a Major Role in the Lives of Some People Who Are Famous in Other Fields."

* * *

Maintain contact with active music educators through the Music Educators National Conference. MENC can furnish you with a forum for talking about music education and can put you in contact with beginning teachers who may be having problems and could profit from your advice and help. Keep your MENC membership and remain active.

* * *

Become acquainted with the MENC publications that can help you in your role as advocate. *Beyond the Classroom: Informing Others* provides many practical ideas about how to reach effectively a wide range of individuals and groups such as the general public, district administrators and school board members, school principals, counselors, parents, the media, the community, arts organizations, and government officials. Read this publication carefully and use the suggestions. With the move to include a comprehensive program of general music in the high school curriculum, the new MENC publication, *Music in the High School: Current Approaches to Secondary General Music Instruction* will be especially helpful to retired music educators who wish to be effective advocates for making high-quality music programs available to *all* high school students.

Become familiar with the set of brochures *Working Together for Quality Music Education for All Students,* published by MENC in conjunction with other education associations including the National School Boards Association, the American Association of School Administrators, the National Congress of Parents and Teachers, and the American Association for Counseling and Development. These brochures contain statements that have been agreed upon by both MENC and the cooperating associations. All of the above publications can be ordered from Publication Sales, MENC, 1902 Association Drive, Reston, Virginia 22091.

* * *

Write articles for the *Music Educators Journal*. Submit articles and contributions to the "Readers Comment," "Point of View," and "Idea Bank" columns. You can obtain a copy of the *MEJ* style guidelines by writing to the Editor, *Music Educators Journal*, at MENC headquarters in Reston.

Attend sessions at MENC national, division, and state conferences where public relations and legislative topics are discussed.

* * *

Write an article on the importance of having high-quality music programs in our educational system for the "In My Opinion" column in your local newspaper. If there is some sentiment in your community that music is not a basic part of education, write a letter to the editor of your local newspaper, explaining why music is indeed an important part of one's education. Your letter to the editor, backed up by your wide experience, can be helpful to the cause of music education.

If the local school administration or school board is contemplating a cutback in the current music program, write a letter of strong protest to the superintendent. Cite the reasons why a cutback will be damaging to the total school program. Send copies of this letter to all members of the school board.

Lead a group of interested citizens in the community in attending the next meeting of the school board and articulate a vigorous protest. Stress the real and important need for maintaining a strong and effective program of music education for all students.

* * *

Support Music In our Schools Month (MIOSM) by working with the local MIOSM chair to help promote the activities offered in connection with this outstanding program. Inform the newspapers and radio and television stations in your community about this endeavor. Volunteer to assist the local MIOSM chair in the development of a city- or area-wide focus on this program.

* * *

When your school system presents an excellent music program, write a letter to the superintendent of schools complimenting all concerned for their exemplary work. Send copies of this letter to the members of the school board and to the director of the program.

* * *

Help develop a strong liaison between the public school music teachers and the private music teachers in your community. Both groups are working toward the same goal: making young Americans musically literate. Recommend to the leaders of each group that one or two formal meetings or informal social gatherings be held jointly each year. The members of both groups may find attending each group's programs and recitals very rewarding. Suggest to school personnel that they send invitations to school programs to the private music teachers. Volunteer to serve as an intermediary between the two groups.

* * *

Contact a member of the state or federal legislature, and ask for his or her assistance in promoting high-quality music programs in the public schools. Have both data and a rationale ready to support your request. Be frank, open, and well-informed, and know your legislator. Ask him or her to write a statement in support of a strong music program as part of a well-balanced program of education in today's schools, an article on the subject for the local newspaper, or a statement about why he or she believes that music is an important part of everyone's life. Invite this legislator to introduce or take part in a music program being presented by an individual school or district. He or she will welcome the exposure and will be impressed with the program.

* * *

It has been wisely said
that whatever many may say about
the future, it is ours,
not only that it may
happen to us, but it is in part
made by us.

Ethel Percy Andrus

* * *

Bibliography

Carlsen, Mary Baird. *Meaning-Making: Therapeutic Processes in Adult Development.* New York: Norton, 1988. (See especially chapter 13, "Creative Aging.")

Downs, Hugh, and Richard J. Roll. *The Best Years Book: How to Plan for Fulfillment, Security, and Happiness in the Retirement Years.* New York: Delacorte Press, 1981.

Gardner, John W. *Excellence.* New York: Harper & Row, 1961.

Kaplan, Max. *Leisure: Lifestyle and Lifespan Perspectives for Gerontology.* Philadelphia: W. B. Saunders, 1979.

LaShan, Eda. *Oh! To Be Fifty Again.* New York: Time Books, 1986.

Mustric, Peter. *The Joy of Growing Older.* Wheaton, IL: Tyndale House, 1979.

National Association of Mature People. *Your Key to the Best Years: A Retirement Guide from the National Association of Mature People.* Oklahoma City, OK: National Association of Mature People, n.d. (2212 Northwest Fiftieth Street, P.O. Box 26792, Oklahoma City, OK 73126)

Sarton, Mae. *At Seventy.* New York: Norton, 1984.

Scott-Maxwell, Florida. *The Measure of My Days.* New York: Knopf, 1968.

Skinner, B. F., and Margaret Vaughn. *Enjoy Old Age: A Program of Self-Management.* New York: Norton, 1983.

Uris, Auren. *Over 50: The Definitive Guide to Retirement.* Radnet, PA: Chilton, 1979.

Acknowledgments

MENC gratefully acknowledges the following educators who contributed to this booklet:

Ruth Brandon	Brentwood, Tennessee
Lucille Couch	Louisville, Kentucky
Howard Doolin	Miami, Florida
Karl D. Ernst	Santa Rosa, California
John C. McManus	Eugene, Oregon
Billie B. Wilson	Beaverton, Oregon

MENC and the compiler also acknowledge the contributions to this booklet by Mary Baird Carlsen, a clinical psychologist in Seattle, who presented sessions for music educators who are retired and about to retire at the 1983 Northwest Division Conference in Seattle and at the 1985 Northwest Division Conference in Spokane, Washington, by Leslie Lareau of the Department of Human Development and Family Ecology at the University of Illinois in Urbana, who presented a session for a similar group of educators at the 1984 national conference of MENC in Chicago, and by Ethel Percy Andrus, founder of AARP and the National Retired Teachers Association. Several suggestions in this booklet are derived from those presentations.